MAY 2017

SandCastle

Rhyme Time

The HuN PlAys ONe-oN-ONe

Anders Hanson

Consulting Editor, Diane Craig, M.A./Reading Specialist

ABDO
Publishing Company

Published by ABDO Publishing Company, 4940 Viking Drive, Edina, Minnesota 55435.

Copyright © 2005 by Abdo Consulting Group, Inc. International copyrights reserved in all countries. No part of this book may be reproduced in any form without written permission from the publisher. SandCastle™ is a trademark and logo of ABDO Publishing Company.

Printed in the United States.

Credits
Edited by: Pam Price
Curriculum Coordinator: Nancy Tuminelly
Cover and Interior Design and Production: Mighty Media
Photo and Illustration Credits: BananaStock Ltd., Brand X Pictures, Digital Vision, Anders Hanson, Hemera, Image Source, PhotoDisc, Rubberball Productions, Stockbyte

Library of Congress Cataloging-in-Publication Data

Hanson, Anders, 1980-
    The Hun plays one-on-one / Anders Hanson.
        p. cm. -- (Rhyme time)
    Includes index.
    ISBN 1-59197-794-0 (hardcover)
    ISBN 1-59197-900-5 (paperback)
    1. English language--Rhyme--Juvenile literature. I. Title. II. Rhyme time (ABDO Publishing Company)

    PE1517.H3754 2004
    808.1--dc22
                                                                              2004049042

SandCastle™ books are created by a professional team of educators, reading specialists, and content developers around five essential components that include phonemic awareness, phonics, vocabulary, text comprehension, and fluency. All books are written, reviewed, and leveled for guided reading, early intervention reading, and Accelerated Reader® programs and designed for use in shared, guided, and independent reading and writing activities to support a balanced approach to literacy instruction.

Let Us Know

After reading the book, SandCastle would like you to tell us your stories about reading. What is your favorite page? Was there something hard that you needed help with? Share the ups and downs of learning to read. We want to hear from you! To get posted on the ABDO Publishing Company Web site, send us e-mail at:

sandcastle@abdopub.com

SandCastle Level: Transitional

Words that rhyme do
not have to be spelled the
same. These words rhyme
with each other:

run

bun

done   son

fun   spun

gun   ton

none   won

Trish and Marian each wear their hair in a bun.

Edward can go out to play when his homework is done.

The girls have **fun** jumping rope.

Jase is looking for a purple puzzle piece, but there are **none**.

Lindy squirts her dad with a water **gun**.

The Randalls have one daughter and one **son**.

The children love to **run** on the beach.

When Don picked up the box,
it felt like it weighed a ton.

Sandra **spun** the hula hoop around her waist.

The girls on the soccer team cheered when they **won**.

The Hun Plays One-On-One

Gorilla the Hun
loves to play one-on-one.

14

But he's so big and mean,
no one wants to have fun
with Gorilla the Hun.

15

No one, that is,
except an itty bitty nun.

"My son," said the nun,
"Let's play one-on-one."

"All right," said the Hun,
"But I'm the meanest player,
and the biggest by a ton!"

After much chatter,
the game was begun.

The Hun weighed in at over a ton.
But the nun was too quick.
Oh, how fast she could run!

She ran so fast that
the Hun's head spun.

After all was said and done,
the itty bitty nun had won!

The final score was 101 to none.

Rhyming Riddle

What do you call a roll that has finished baking?

Done bun

Glossary

beach. a sandy or pebbly shore of a body of water

bun. a roll of hair fastened to the back of the head; a small bread roll

hula hoop. a plastic hoop that is twirled around the body

hun. a mean and destructive person

nun. a woman who belongs to a religious group and lives in a convent

one-on-one. having only one player on each team

ton. a common expression for *a lot*

About SandCastle™

A professional team of educators, reading specialists, and content developers created the SandCastle™ series to support young readers as they develop reading skills and strategies and increase their general knowledge. The SandCastle™ series has four levels that correspond to early literacy development in young children. The levels are provided to help teachers and parents select the appropriate books for young readers.

Emerging Readers
(no flags)

Beginning Readers
(1 flag)

Transitional Readers
(2 flags)

Fluent Readers
(3 flags)

These levels are meant only as a guide. All levels are subject to change.

To see a complete list of SandCastle™ books and other nonfiction titles from ABDO Publishing Company, visit www.abdopub.com or contact us at:
4940 Viking Drive, Edina, Minnesota 55435 • 1-800-800-1312 • fax: 1-952-831-1632